This book of New York Doodles belongs to:

_____

Book Design: Susan Bogle and David Turner

First Edition

ISBN: 978-0-9838121-3-5

Printed in China

CPSIA Compliance Information: Batch #033013DP
For further information contact Duo Press, LLC at info@duopressbooks.com

duopress
www.duopressbooks.com

DOODLE
New York

By Puck • Illustrations by Violet Lemay

duopress

Ready?

Go!

Welcome to New York!
Doodle your own Big Apple!

Draw a **rain shower** over the **city.**

Now, it's **sunny.** Doodle a **rainbow.**

How about some **hot-air balloons?**

It's getting late. **New York** needs some **stars!**

Draw some **straphangers** on the **subway**.

Straphangers is a nickname
for subway riders in New York.

What's **your** favorite **baseball team?**

Color this **coffee cup.**

This paper coffee cup is known as the Anthora.

Now, draw your own cup.

The **Flatiron Building** needs some **windows.**

Scan this QR code
to get coloring pages
made by Graham Fruisen,
a kid just like you!

Draw some butterflies.

If you like butterflies you can see
many kinds at the Butterfly Garden
at the Bronx Zoo.

Draw your favorite
Broadway show.

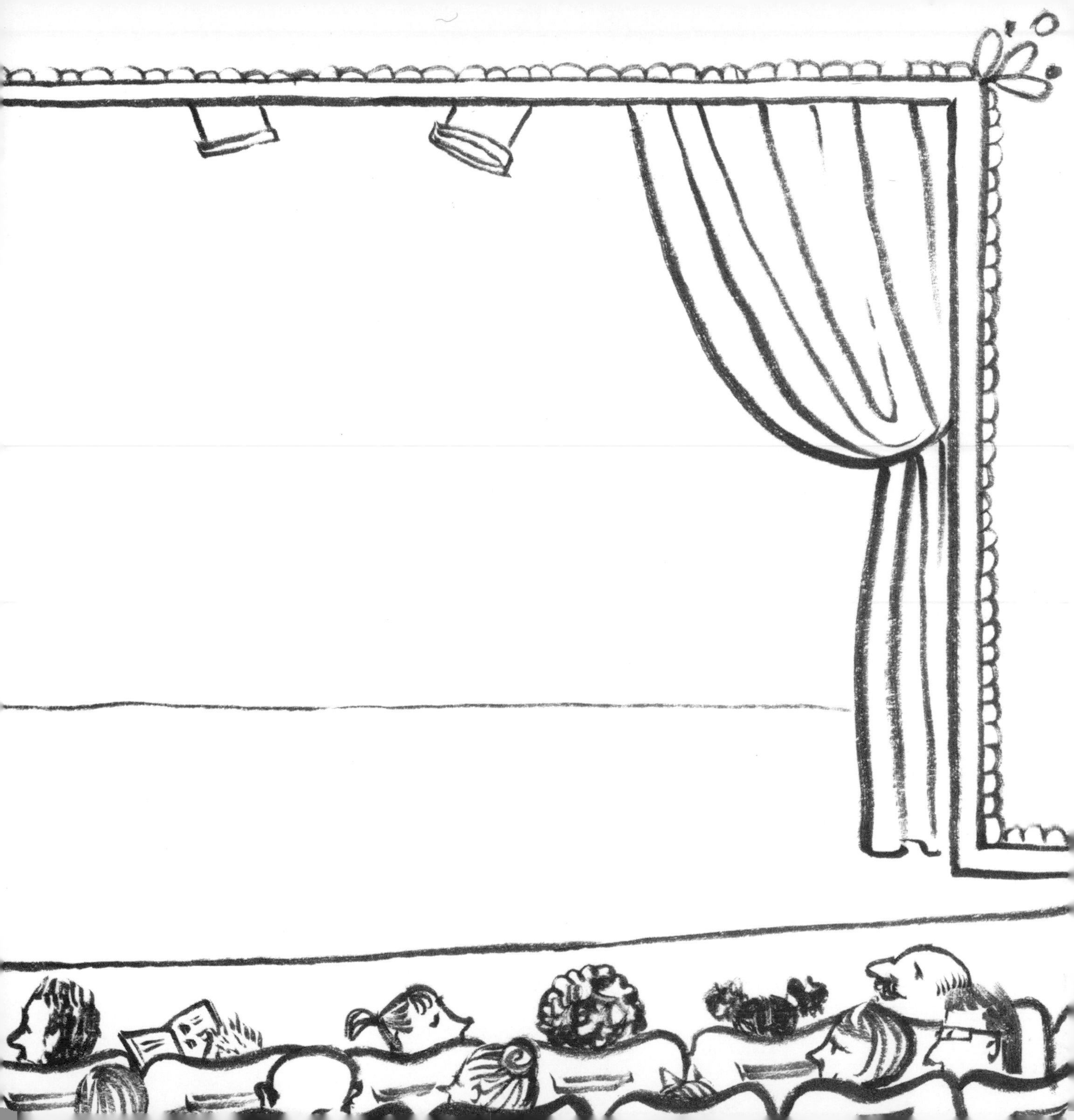

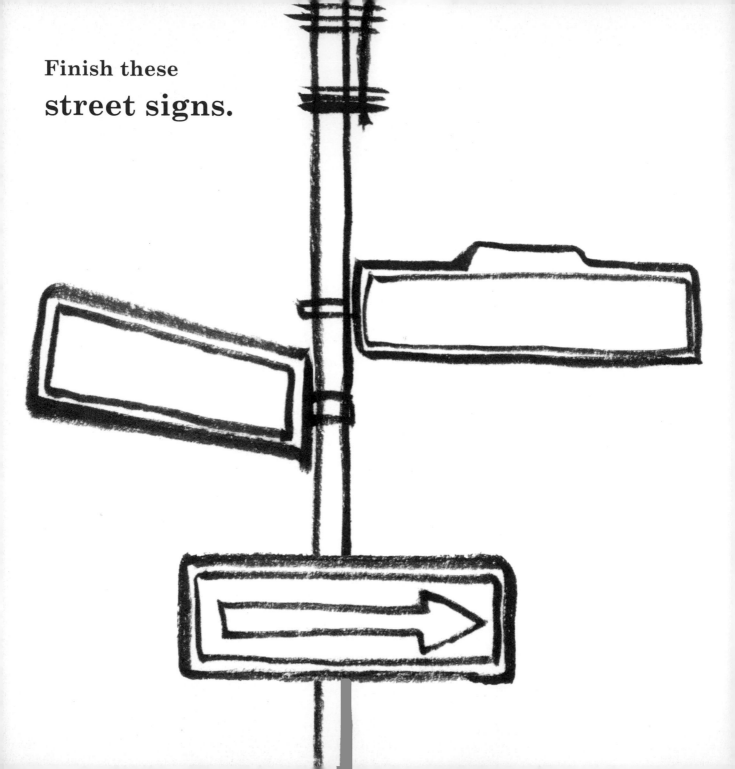

Finish these
street signs.

Who is in the
spotlight?

These **people crossing** the street need **faces.**

This **snow globe** needs some **buildings.**

Finish this dinosaur.

Meet the dinosaurs at the Fossil Halls
in the American Museum of Natural History.

Color the **sign**
of the **Apollo Theater.**

The famous Apollo Theater is located in Harlem.

Fill these **baskets** at the **farmers' market.**

Decorate this **T-shirt.**

Scan this and get more
T-shirts to color!

Now **doodle** your own **T-shirt.**

Color some **poison frogs.**
Use lots of **colors.**

A great place to see poison frogs (and other slimy animals) is at the World of Reptiles in the Bronx Zoo.

Doodle some jellyfish.

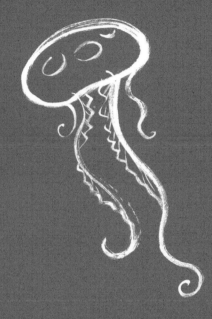

You have to check out these extraordinary
aquatic creatures at the New York
Aquarium, in Coney Island, Brooklyn.

Doodle a few **penguins.**

Doodle a **parakeet.**

Meet a parakeet, and many other
fantastic birds, at the Aviary in the Queens Zoo.

What time is it?

New York's most
famous clock, at
Grand Central Station.

Finish the
Statue of Liberty

This **pedicab** needs a **driver**.

Take the **Doodle Challenge:**
Draw an **apple** using **one single line.**

Look for 4 more Doodle Challenges ahead!

Color the lights on the Empire State Building.

Christmas

Independence Day

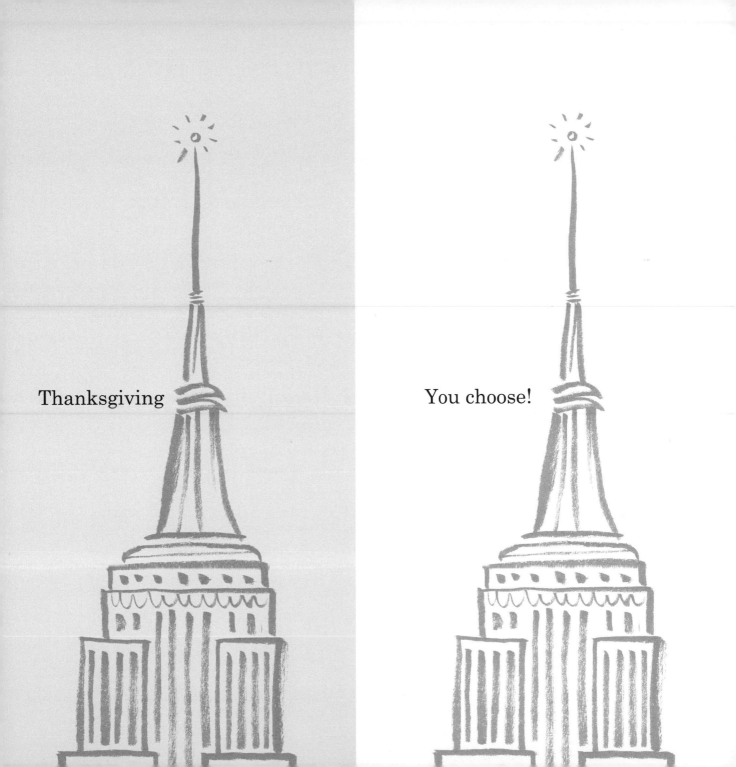

Thanksgiving

You choose!

Doodle the **CRAZIEST** thing you've seen
in **New York!**

Doodle a **BIG**
cockroach.

Doodle the **passengers** in this **bus.**

Now, doodle your own **bus.**

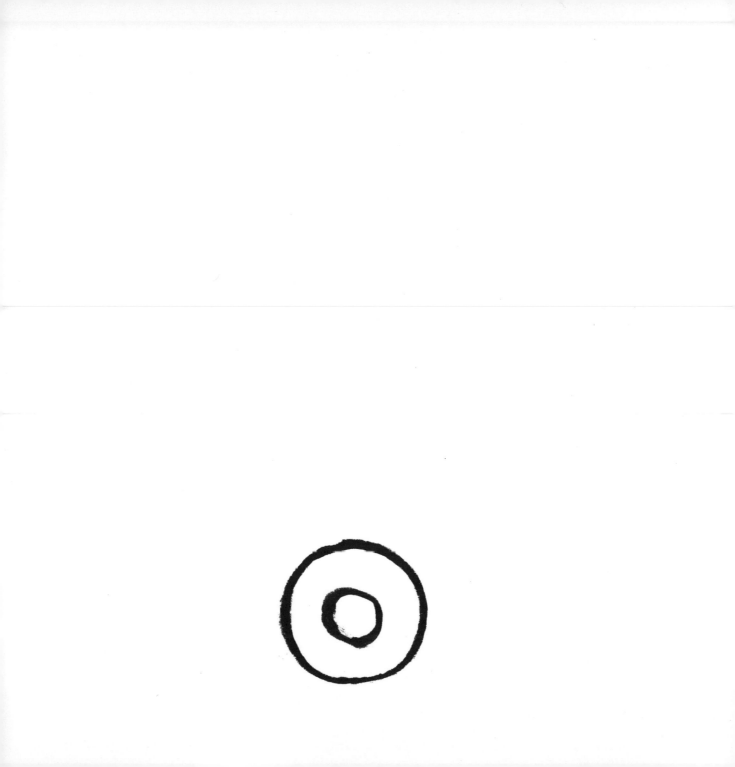

This **messenger** needs a **bicycle.**

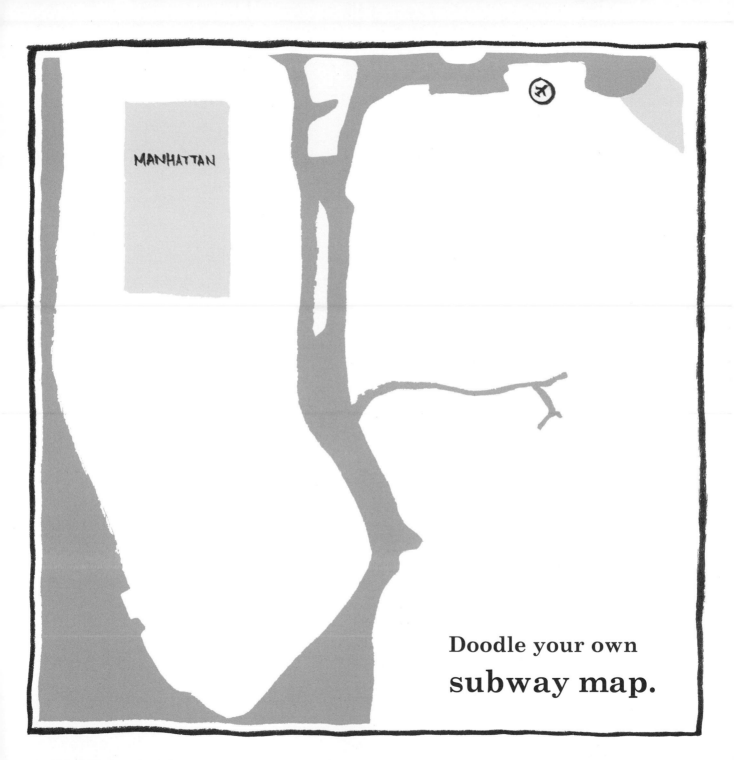

MANHATTAN

Doodle your own
subway map.

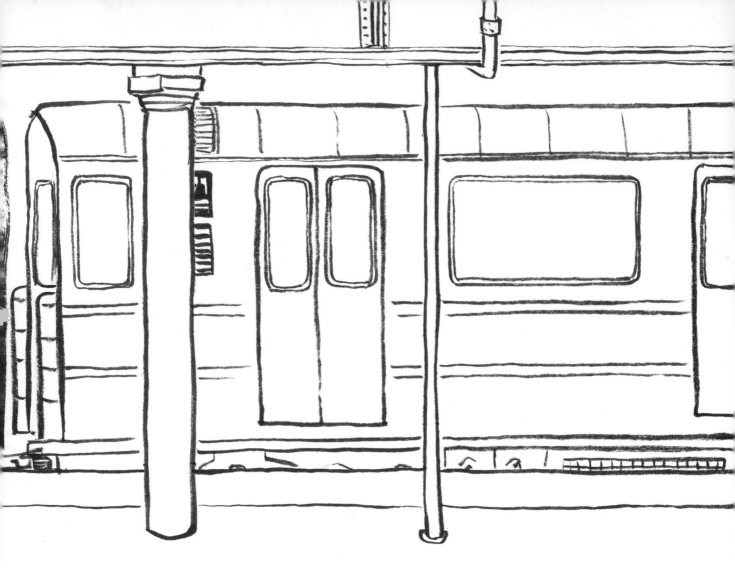

Doodle the **passengers** on the **subway**.

It's **Fashion Week.** Help these **models** with **their makeup!**

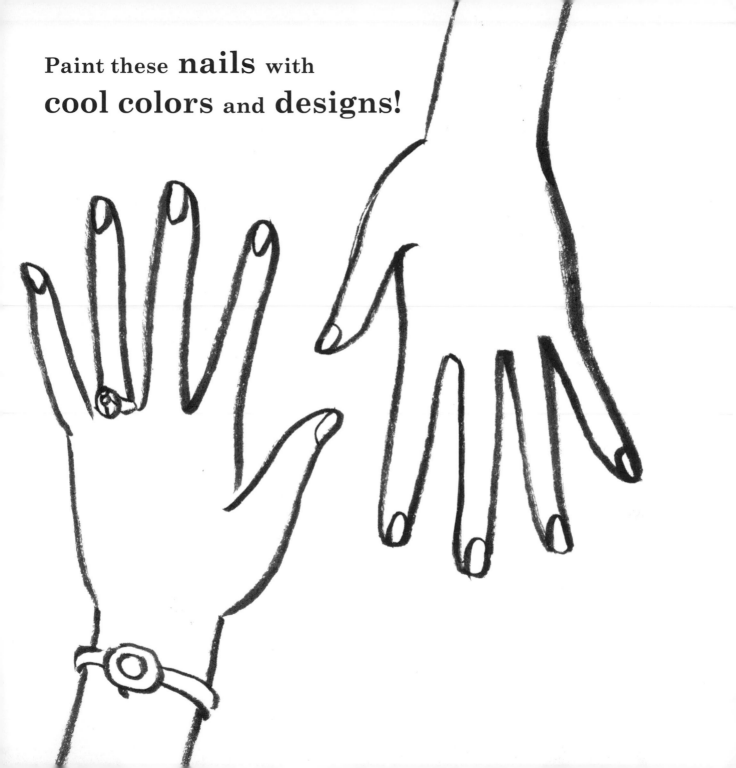

Paint these **nails** with **cool colors** and **designs!**

Doodle some **shopping bags.**

Design your own **sneaker.**

Scan this and get more
cool shoes to color!

Draw the cover of your own book.

Take the **Doodle Challenge:**
Draw an **apple** with your **eyes closed.**

Look for 3 more Doodle Challenges ahead!

Finish the **George Washington** Bridge.

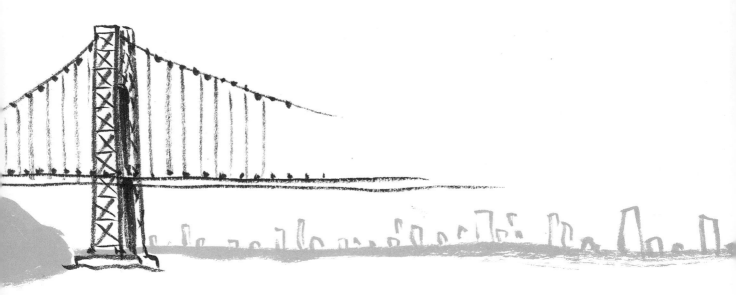

The George Washington Bridge connects
New York with New Jersey.

Doodle the **name and number** of your favorite **New York Yankee.**

Doodle the **name** and **number** of your favorite **New York Met.**

Fill this **box** with your **favorite**
kind of **pizza**.

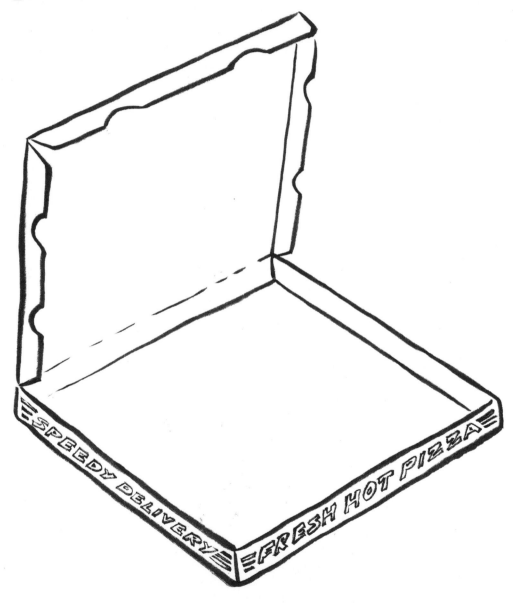

Decorate these **cupcakes.** Use lots of **colors!**

Finish this **hotdog** cart.

Scan this and get more
NY foods to color!

This **food truck** needs a **name,** a **menu,** and your **favorite food!**

What's your **favorite** kind of **bagel?**

Take the **Doodle Challenge:**
Draw an **apple** with your **left hand**
(Especially if you are **right-handed!).**

Look for 2 more Doodle Challenges ahead!

It's the **4th of July!** Doodle some **fireworks.**

Everybody is waiting in line.

Lady Liberty needs a **crown.**

These **buildings** need **fire escapes.**

These **fire escapes** need **buildings.**

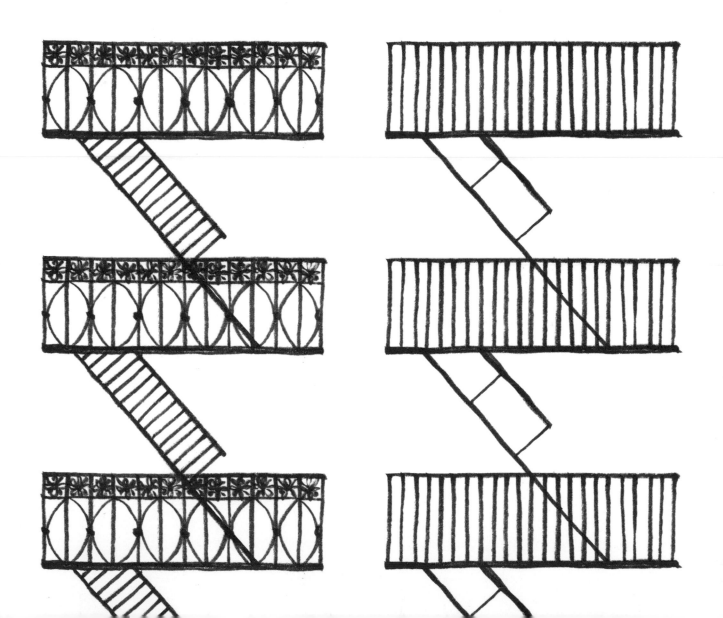

Doodle some sunbathers.

What's your favorite beach in New York?

Who is winning the New York City Marathon?

Doodle the **name** and **number** of your favorite **New York Giant.**

Doodle the **name** and **number** of your favorite **New York Jet.**

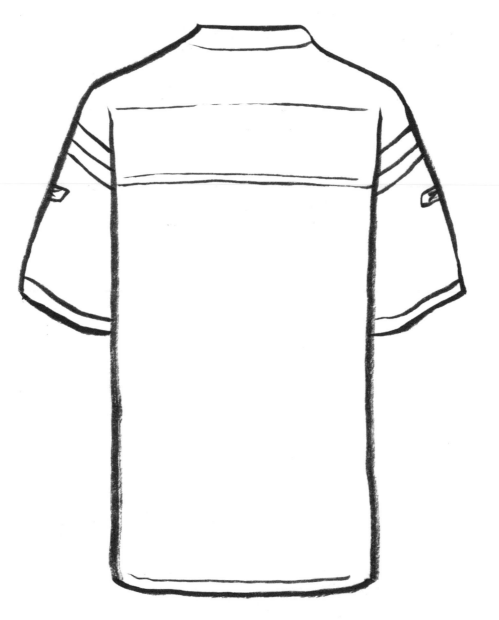

Doodle your own **modern** masterpiece.

Spot some masterpieces at the
Museum of Modern Art (MoMA).

Now, doodle your own **modern** sculpture.

Here are some **bonsai trees.** Can you draw some **leaves** on them?

These trees are waiting for you at the C.V. Starr Bonsai Museum in the Brooklyn Botanical Garden.

It's the **Orchid Show!**
Doodle some **pretty orchids.**

If you like orchids, the Orchid Show at the New York Botanical Garden is the place for you!

Doodle a **float** for the
Thanksgiving Parade.

Now, make your own parade!

It's **Halloween.** Who is wearing these **hats?**

A great place to celebrate Halloween is at
New York's Village Halloween Parade.

Now doodle **Halloween hats** on these **people!**

Take the Doodle Challenge:

Draw an **apple** with your **right hand** (Especially if you are **left-handed!**).

Look for 1 more Doodle Challenge ahead!

Finish this **storefront.**

This **stage** needs some **classic dancers.**

If you like dance, you will love the New York City Ballet.

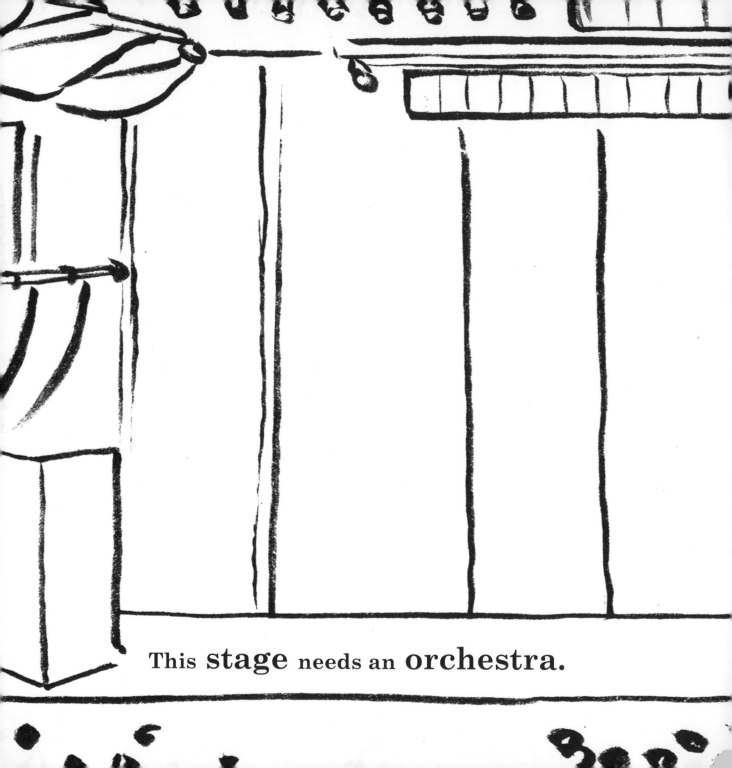

This **stage** needs an **orchestra**.

This is the stage at Avery Fisher Hall in Lincoln Center.

Doodle some **visitors** at the **High Line.**

Can you doodle a
marble lion
in front of the New York
Public Library?

Doodle some people walking across the Brooklyn Bridge.

The Brooklyn Bridge connects Brooklyn with Manhattan.

What's your **favorite** football **team?**

Doodle the **name** and **number** of your favorite **New York Knick.**

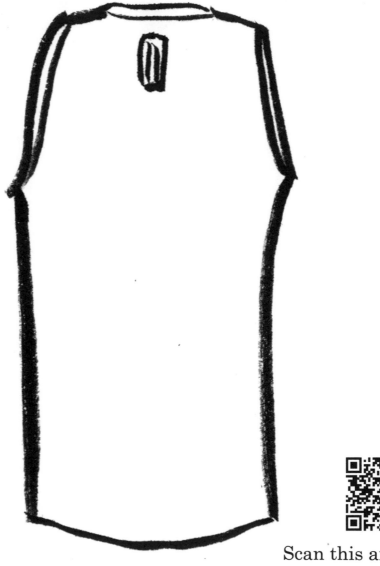

Scan this and get more jerseys to color!

Take the Doodle Challenge:

Draw an **apple** with **one** single line using your **two hands!**

Decorate these **flags.**

Color the
Christmas tree
in **Rockefeller**
Center.

Doodle some riders on the Staten Island ferry.

The Staten Island ferry cruises from Lower Manhattan to Staten Island.

Finish this doodle of the Space Shuttle *Enterprise*.

The Intrepid Sea, Air & Space Museum has some super cool flying, and floating, machines!

USA

This **fireman** needs his **uniform.**

Scan this and get more
NY characters to color!

Where is the doorman?
Can you doodle **him?**

This **person** needs a **dog.**

Can you finish this **armor?**

Cool pieces of armor, like this one, are on display at the Arms and Armor Collection in the Metropolitan Museum of Art.

Can you doodle the **Guggenheim Museum?**
Use the sample as **inspiration.**

Doodle some **constellations** in the sky.

The Hayden Planetarium at the American Museum of Natural History is a good place to explore the stars!

Doodle some pigeons.

Doodle your own taxi.

Doodle the **tramway** going to **Roosevelt Island.**

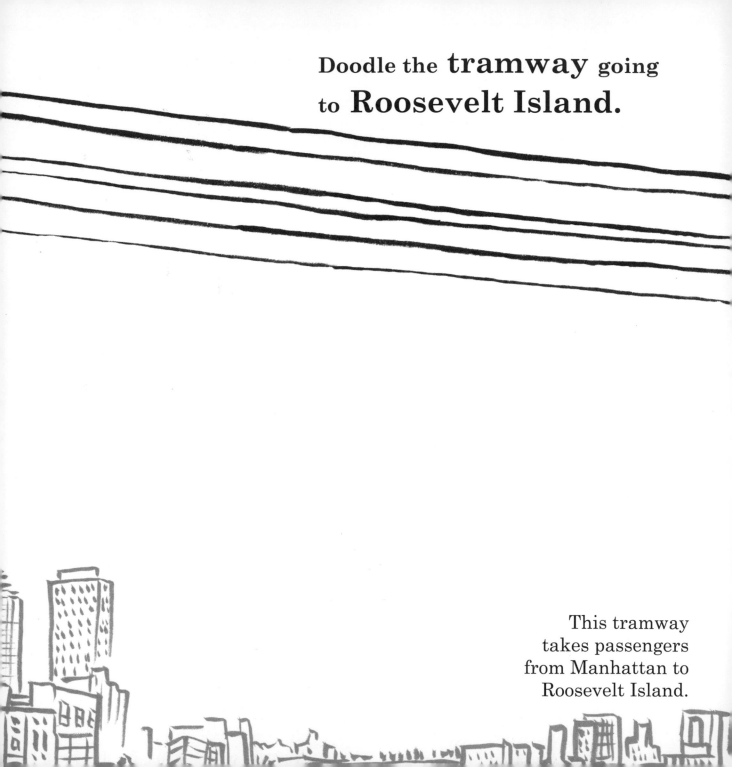

This tramway takes passengers from Manhattan to Roosevelt Island.

These **buildings** need **water towers.**

Draw some **cars** crossing
the **Verrazano Bridge.**

The Verrazano-Narrows Bridge connects the
boroughs of Staten Island and Brooklyn.

Doodle your own **circus act.**

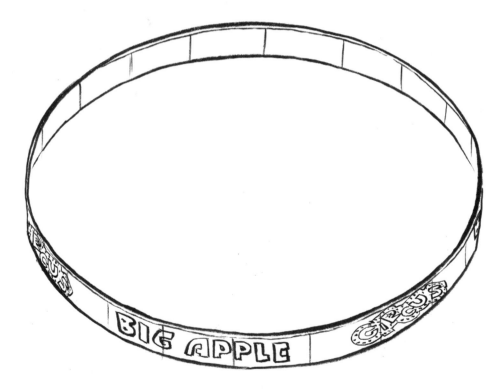

Have you ever seen the Big Apple Circus?

This **deli** needs some **flowers.**

Fill your **photo album** with **memories** of New York.

Can you doodle the top of the Chrysler Building?